Name

_____

Contact Info

_____

_____

_____

If you don't have any goals,
make your first goal
"getting some goals."

MELODY BEATTIE

Getting Started

This simple little journal has big potential. The dot grid can be used for the usual journaling purposes—for sketching, doodling, planning, scrapbooking, keeping prayer lists, whatever it is you put in your journal. It has been built, however, to be used as a bullet journal. Bullet journaling is an organizational system allowing you to include all of the above in a do-it-yourself planning journal that keeps you mindful of what is important to you.

How does it work? There is an index in the front, and the pages are numbered throughout. You can put poetry on page 7, your weekly calendar on page 8, and menus with recipes on page 9. Jot down the page numbers in the index and you will easily find your latest poem, grocery list, or what you have planned for dinner. Most planners have a set number of pages for your schedule. Sometimes there are several pages in a row with nothing on them because you were too busy to write or just weren't feeling inspired. With this journal, you don't have to be that linear (but if that works for you, build it that way). A month can fill six pages or sixty. It is up to you. Fill the pages with words, art, calendars, or movie ticket stubs. Your journal. Your choice.

What makes this different than other bullet journals? There are meaningful quotes and Bible verses sprinkled throughout to inspire and encourage you. They are unobtrusive prompts to go deeper in your daily planning to include faith steps and prayer time. But they take up very little real estate on the page.

If you search the Internet, you will find a plethora of ideas on how to personalize your bullet journal. There are modules showing you how to make yearly, monthly, and daily calendars, add favorite Scripture, art, or keep track of your to-do list like a pro. You can keep it straightforward and simple or add lettering and color to create a one-of-a-kind work of art.

Whichever way you personalize it, use it daily. Even five minutes a day can make a big difference in your life, especially if you are pairing it with meaningful time with God. Plan and pray, and you will find there is a time for every purpose.

INDEX

INDEX

INDEX

Slow down awhile! Push aside the press of the immediate. < GARY SMALLEY AND JOHN TRENT

Make today so fabulous that all the other days are jealous.

A good deed is never lost; he who sows courtesy reaps friendship, and he who plants kindness gathers love.
< Basil of Caesarea

Influence, just like salt shaken out, is hard to see, but its flavor is hard to miss. < PAM FARREL

I still find each day too short for all the thoughts I want to think. < JOHN BURROUGHS   55

To feel rich, count all the things you have that money can't buy.

Goodness is the only investment that never fails. < HENRY DAVID THOREAU

Looking forward to things is half the pleasure of them. < LUCY MAUD MONTGOMERY

Think of whatever you are doing as an adventure and watch your life change for the better.
< WILFERD A. PETERSON

May God give you the power to accomplish all the good things your faith prompts you to do.
< THE BIBLE

A strong positive mental attitude will create more miracles than any wonder drug. < PATRICIA NEAL

If I cannot do great things, I can do small things in a great way.

The successful [person] will profit from mistakes and try again in a different way. < DALE CARNEGIE

Let us run with endurance the race that is set before us. < THE BIBLE

People with goals succeed because they know where they're going. < EARL NIGHTINGALE

Ellie Claire® Gift & Paper Expressions
Franklin, TN 37067
EllieClaire.com
Ellie Claire is a registered trademark of Worthy Media, Inc.

A Time for Every Purpose Bullet Journal
© 2017 by Ellie Claire
Published by Ellie Claire, an imprint of Worthy Publishing Group, a division of Worthy Media, Inc.

ISBN 978-1-63326-164-8

Stock or custom editions of Ellie Claire titles may be purchased in bulk for educational, business, ministry, fund-raising, or sales promotional use. For information, please e-mail info@EllieClaire.com

Cover art: Creative Market/Lila Chevnenko
Cover design by Melissa Reagan
Interior design and typesetting by Jeff Jansen | AestheticSoup.net

Printed in China

2 3 4 5 6 7 8 9 10 – 21 20 19 18 17